CONTENTS

This collection of Gershwin songs has been specially arranged for players between about Grade I and Grade V standard. The pieces are set out approximately in order of increasing difficulty—the first few are very easy and playable by a virtual beginner; other notes and more complex rhythms are introduced as progressively as the music will allow. A separate clarinet part is included.

PAUL HARRIS

1. FUNNY FACE

(Funny Face)

Printed in Great Britain
OXFORD UNIVERSITY PRESS, MUSIC DEPARTMENT, GREAT CLARENDON STREET, OXFORD OX2 6DP

2. SWANEE
(Capitol Revue)

3. A FOGGY DAY
(A Damsel in Distress)

Bright but warm

4. 'S WONDERFUL
(Funny Face)

5. SUMMERTIME
(Porgy and Bess)

6. THE MAN I LOVE

(Lady, be good!)

* Played: [notation] etc.

7. OH, LADY BE GOOD!

(Lady, be good!)

8. EMBRACEABLE YOU
(Girl Crazy)

9. SWEET AND LOW-DOWN
(Tip-toes)

10. LOVE WALKED IN
(The Goldwyn Follies)

Slowly, with much expression

11. DO, DO, DO
(Oh, Kay!)

12. NICE WORK IF YOU CAN GET IT
(A Damsel in Distress)

13. FASCINATING RHYTHM
(Lady, be good!)

14. IT AIN'T NECESSARILY SO

(Porgy and Bess)

15. I GOT RHYTHM
(Girl Crazy)

Lively, with abandon

Printed in England by Caligraving Limited Thetford Norfolk